SCHIRMER'S LIBRARY
OF MUSICAL CLASSICS

JOHANN FRIEDRICH BURGMÜLLER

Collected Studies for Piano
Op. 100, 105, 109

For Piano

Edited and fingered by Louis Oesterle

G. SCHIRMER, Inc.

7777 W. BLUEMOUND RD. P.O. BOX 13819 MILWAUKEE, WI 53213

www.halleonard.com

CONTENTS

Twenty-five Progressive Studies, Op. 100, Books I and II

Twelve Brilliant and Melodious Studies, Op. 105, Books I and II

Eighteen Characteristic Studies, Op. 109, Books I and II

Twenty-five Easy and Progressive Studies
Op. 100, Books I and II

La candeur
(Frankness)

Edited and Fingered by Louis Oesterle

Johann Friedrich Burgmüller
(1806–1874)

L'arabesque

6

La pastorale

NExt week innocence next page ->

practise both hands!

La petite réunion
(The Little Party)

Allegro, ma non troppo

Innocence

Progrès
(Progress)

Le courant limpide
(The Limpid Stream)

La gracieuse
(Grace)

La chasse
(The Chase)

Allegro vivace ($\bullet$ = 132)

Tendre fleur
(Tender Blossom)

La bergeronnette

(The Wagtail)

L'adieu
(The Farewell)

Consolation

La styrienne

Ballade

21

Douce plainte
(Tender Grieving)

La babillarde

(The Chatterbox)

Inquiétude
(Concern)

Ave Maria

La tarentelle

(Tarantella)

Allegro vivo (♩. = 160)

L'harmonie des anges
(Harmony of the Angels)

Barcarolle

Le retour
(The Return)

L'hirondelle
(The Swallow)

La chevaleresque
(Spirit of Chivalry)

Twelve Brilliant and Melodious Studies
Op. 105, Books I and II

Edited and Fingered by Louis Oesterle

Johann Friedrich Burgmüller
(1806–1874)

40

42

44

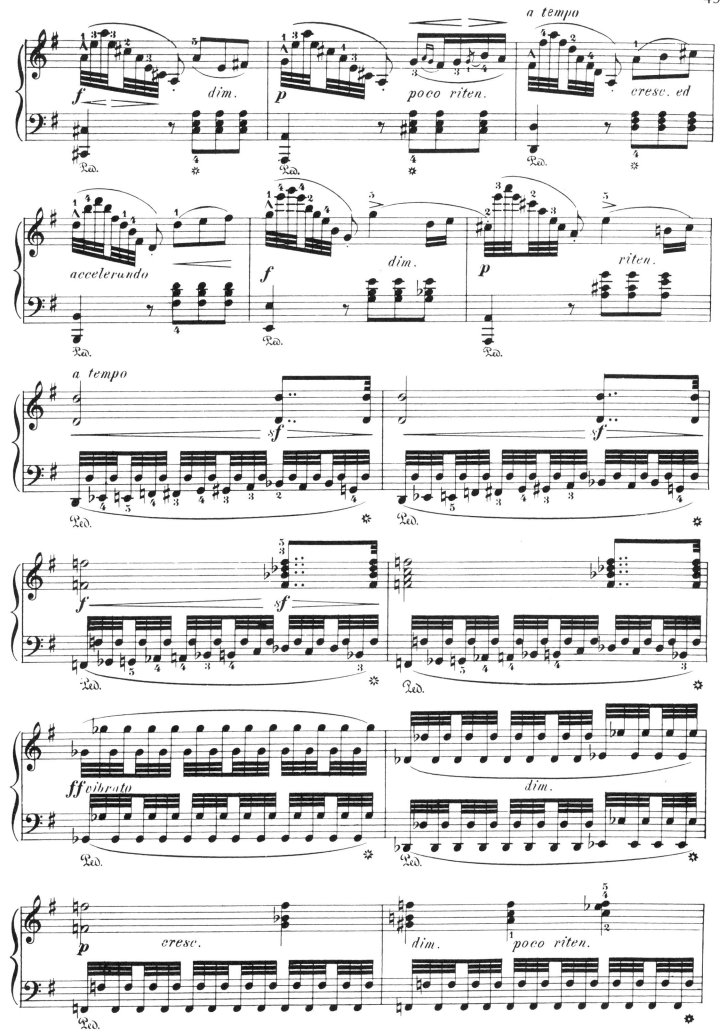

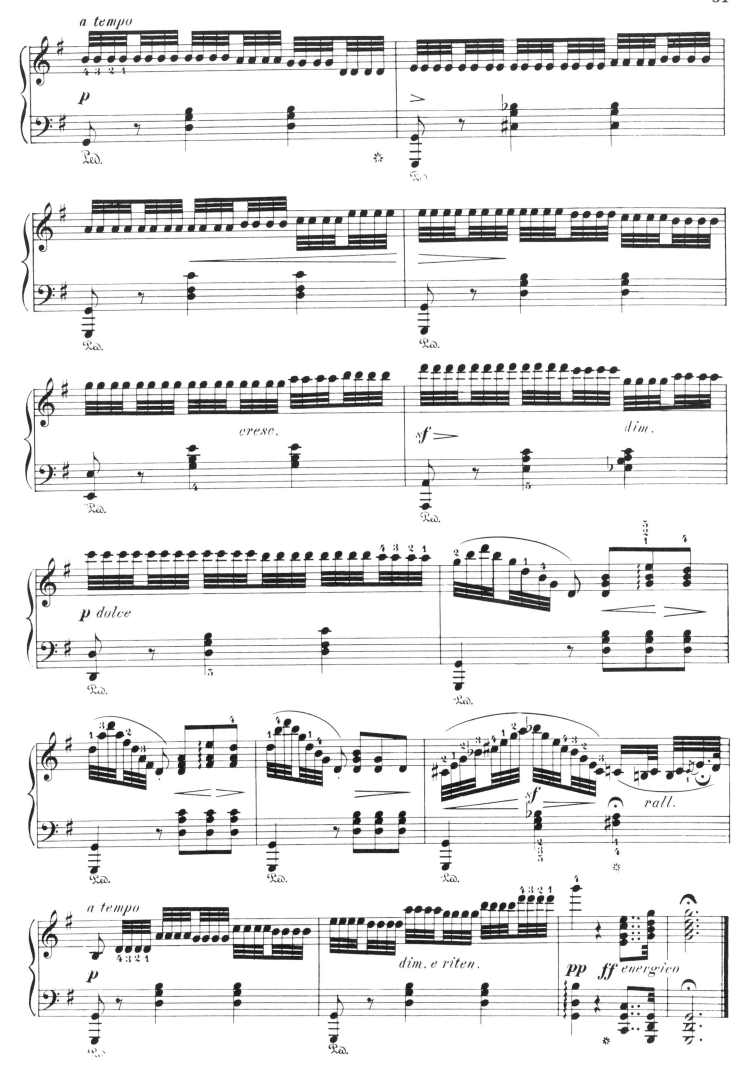

52

56

Allegro non troppo. (♩ = 88)

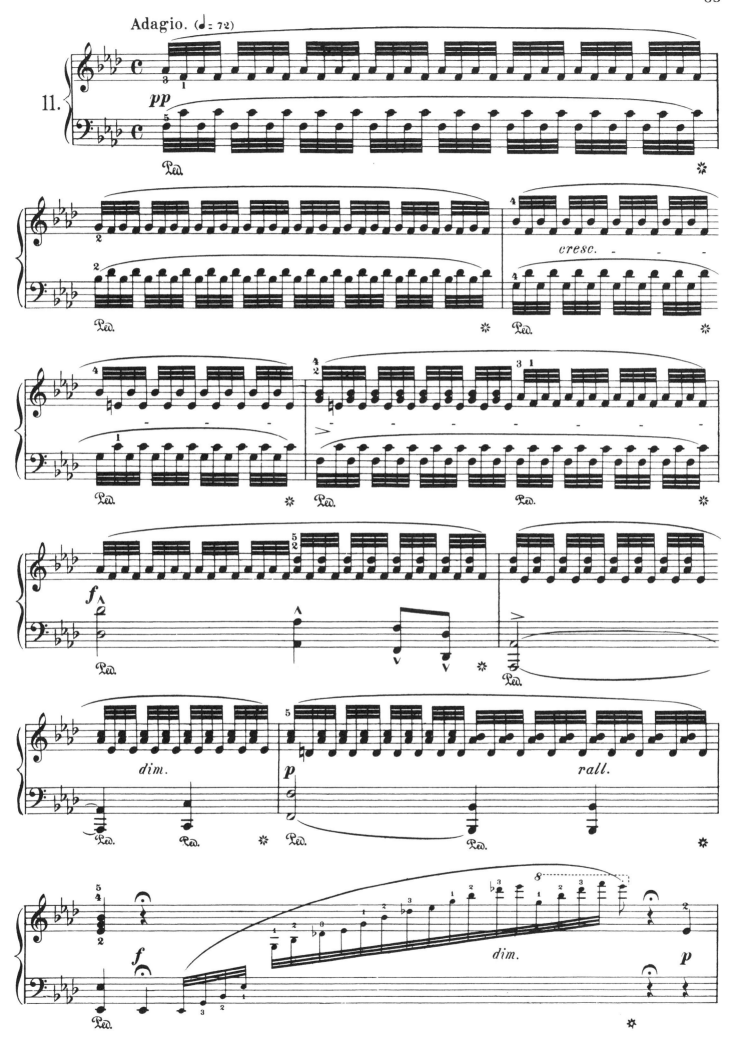

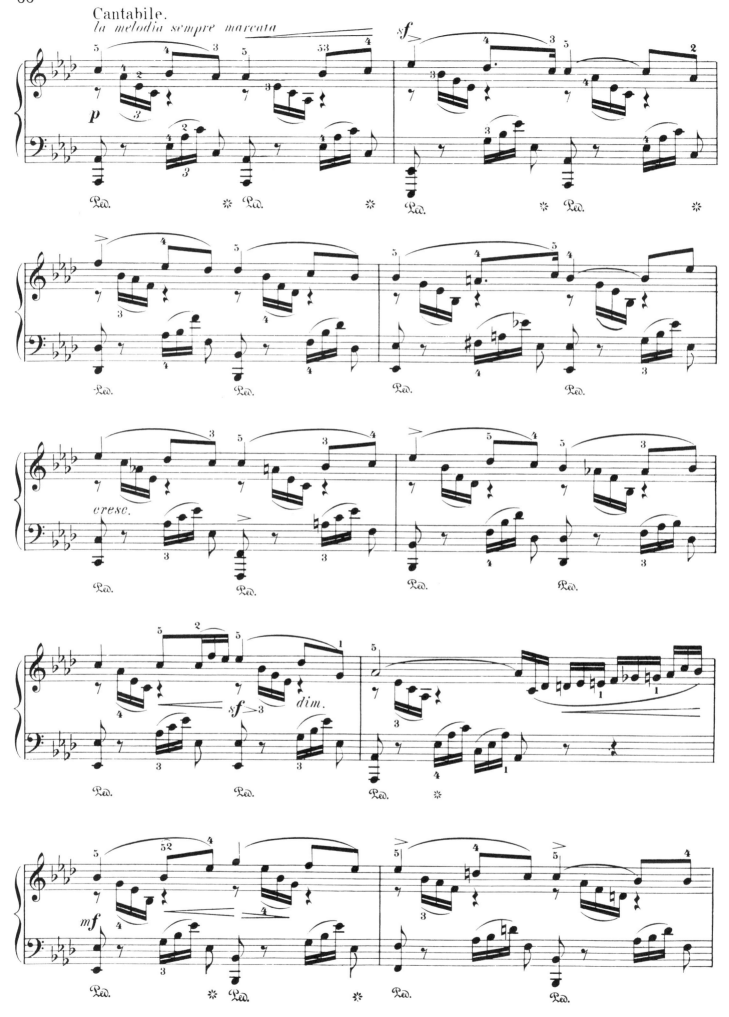

68

Eighteen Characteristic Studies

Op. 109, Books I and II

Confidence

Edited and Fingered by Louis Oesterle

Johann Friedrich Burgmüller
(1806–1874)

Allegro non troppo. (♩ = 152)

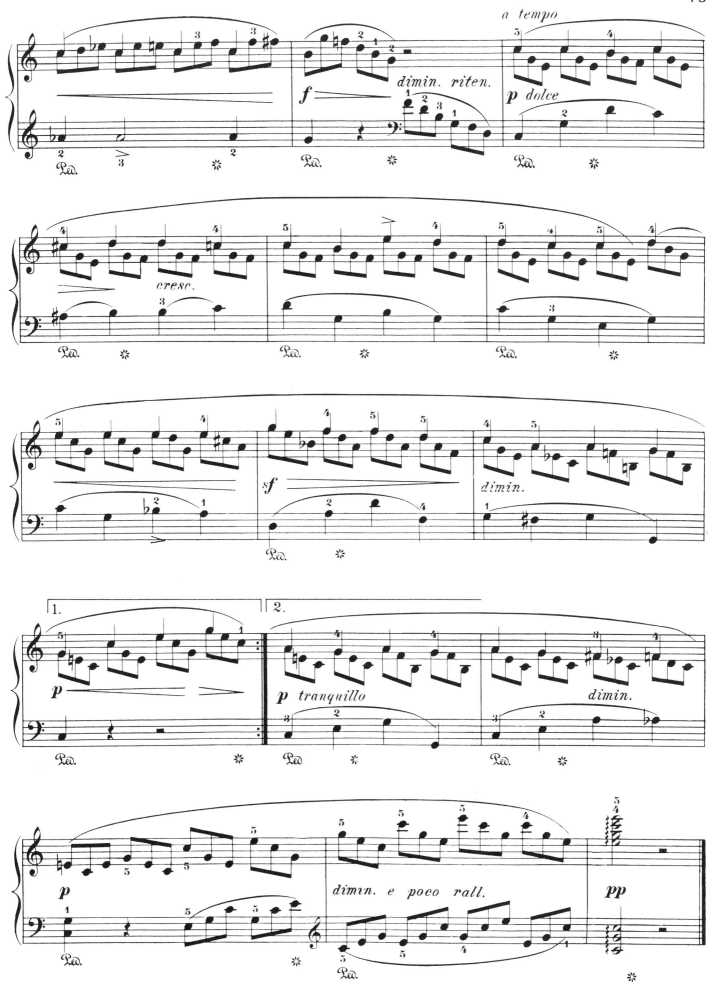

Les perles
(The Pearls)

Le retour du pâtre
(The Shepherd's Return)

Les bohémiens
(The Gypsies)

La source
(The Spring)

Andante grazioso. (♪ = 120)

L'enjouée
(The Light-hearted Maiden)

Berceuse
(Lullaby)

Agitato

La cloche des matines
(The Matin Bell)

La vélocité
(Velocity)

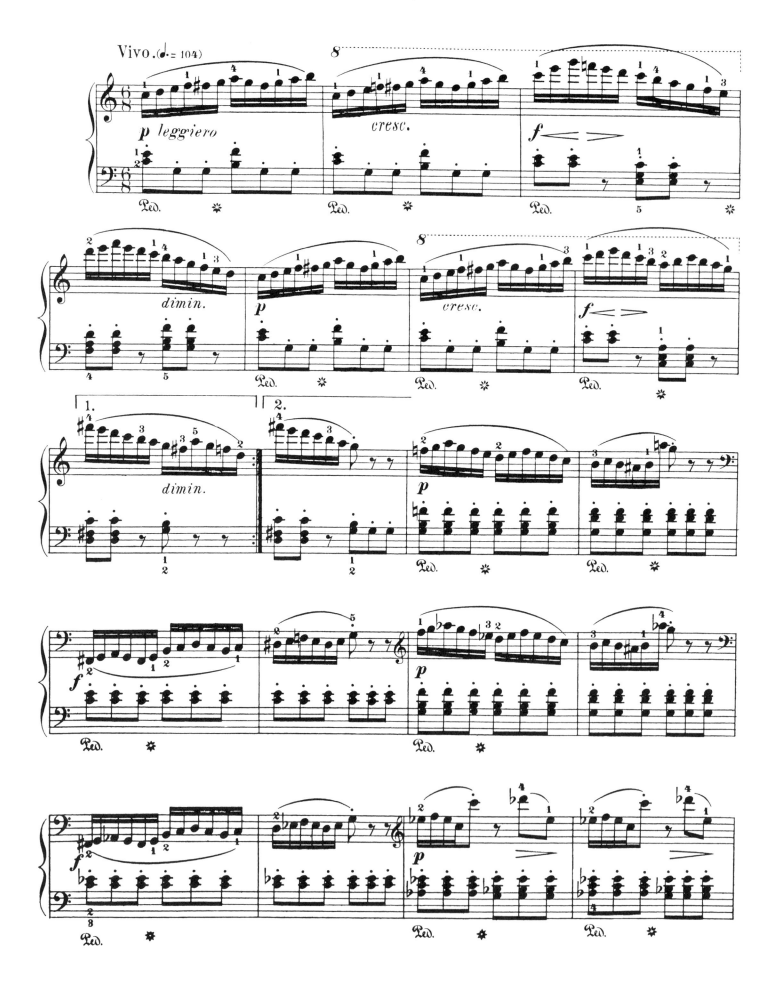

La sérénade
(Serenade)

Le réveil dans les bois
(Awakening in the Woods)

L'orage
(The Storm)

This étude may serve as an introduction to the next.

Refrain du gondolier

(The Gondolier's Refrain)

Les sylphes
(Sylphs)

La séparation
(Parting)

Marche
(March)

La fileuse
(At the Spinning Wheel)